GROUND BREAKERS
BLACK MOVIE MAKERS

AVA DUVERNAY

by Joyce Markovics
and Alrick A. Brown

 CHERRY LAKE PRESS
cherrylakepublishing.com

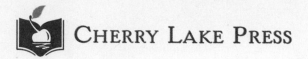

CHERRY LAKE PRESS

Published in the United States of America by Cherry Lake Publishing Group
Ann Arbor, Michigan
www.cherrylakepublishing.com

Reading Adviser: Beth Walker Gambro, MS, Ed., Reading Consultant, Yorkville, IL
Content Adviser: Alrick A. Brown, Film Professor and Filmmaker
Book Designer: Ed Morgan

Photo Credits: © DFree/Shutterstock, cover and title page; © DFree/Shutterstock, 5; © PA Images/Alamy Stock Photo, 6; © Matt Gush/Shutterstock, 7; Wikimedia Commons, 8 © Heidi Besen/Shutterstock, 9; Wikimedia Commons, 10; Mariemaye/Wikimedia Commons, 11 top; freepik.com, 11 bottom; © hurricanehank/Shutterstock, 12; © CELADOR FILMS/Album/Newscom, 13; © FS2/Mandatory Credit: FayesVision/WENN/Newscom, 14; Travis Wise/Wikimedia Commons, 15; © CELADOR FILMS/Album/Newscom, 16; © taniavolobueva/Shutterstock, 17; © Stephen Smith/Sipa USA/Newscom, 18; © DFree/Shutterstock, 19 top; Wikimedia Commons, 19 bottom; © Cubankite/Shutterstock, 21.

Library of Congress Cataloging-in-Publication Data

Names: Markovics, Joyce L. author. | Brown, Alrick, author.
Title: Ava DuVernay / by Joyce Markovics and Alrick A. Brown.
Description: Ann Arbor : Cherry Lake Publishing, 2023. | Series:
  Groundbreakers: black moviemakers | Includes bibliographical references
  and index. | Audience: Grades 4-6
Identifiers: LCCN 2022039528 (print) | LCCN 2022039529 (ebook) | ISBN
  9781668919767 (hardcover) | ISBN 9781668920787 (paperback) | ISBN
  9781668923443 (adobe pdf) | ISBN 9781668922118 (ebook) | ISBN
  9781668924778 (kindle edition)
Subjects: LCSH: DuVernay, Ava—Juvenile literature. | Motion picture
  producers and directors—United States—Biography—Juvenile literature.
  | African American motion picture producers and
  directors—Biography—Juvenile literature. | Women motion picture
  producers and directors—United States—Biography—Juvenile literature.
Classification: LCC PN1998.3.D9255 M37 2023 (print) | LCC PN1998.3.D9255
  (ebook) | DDC 791.4302/33092 [B]—dc23/eng/20221103
LC record available at https://lccn.loc.gov/2022039528
LC ebook record available at https://lccn.loc.gov/2022039529

CONTENTS

THIS IS AVA

"IF YOUR DREAM IS ONLY ABOUT YOU, IT'S TOO SMALL."
—AVA DUVERNAY

Filmmaker Ava DuVernay is an unstoppable force. She makes movies about the experiences of Black people and issues that affect Black communities. An **activist** with a camera, Ava believes in "fighting for **justice**, fighting for good." Since 2008, she has risen to become one of the top Black women moviemakers today. Ava is a leader and inspiration to other filmmakers of color. And this groundbreaker is still going strong.

Ava DuVernay is best known for her work about Black Americans.

Ava became the first African American woman to win the best director award at the Sundance Film Festival. Sundance is one of the most respected film festivals in the world.

EARLY LIFE

"DON'T WAIT FOR PERMISSION TO DO SOMETHING CREATIVE."
—AVA DUVERNAY

On August 24, 1972, Ava DuVernay was born in Long Beach, California. She was raised by her mother, Darlene, and her stepfather. Ava had four siblings. "We lived in Compton, and my mother sometimes didn't want us to go outside," Ava said. "So we would stay inside and create whole worlds." Young Ava loved using her imagination.

Ava and her mom, Darlene Maye

Ava was close to her Aunt Denise who taught her about art. "That was a huge influence on me," said Ava. She and her aunt watched movies together, including *West Side Story* (1961). Ava learned the power of film. And Ava's mom taught her that art could have an impact. "Say something through the arts," her mother would say.

Compton, California, in the 1970s where Ava grew up

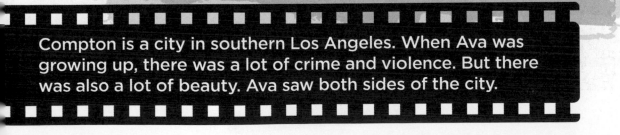

Compton is a city in southern Los Angeles. When Ava was growing up, there was a lot of crime and violence. But there was also a lot of beauty. Ava saw both sides of the city.

Ava's birth father, Joseph, was from Alabama. She would spend summers there, not far from the city of Selma. In 1965, before Ava was born, Ava's father saw activists marching from Selma to Montgomery, Alabama. They were led by Dr. Martin Luther King Jr. The people peacefully marched against injustice. At the time, Black people did not have equal rights in America, especially in the South. They faced harsh rules called Jim Crow laws. Ava's father talked to his daughter about injustice and the civil rights movement. These conversations would later inspire Ava's films.

Dr. Martin Luther King Jr. was a powerful civil rights leader from Alabama. He fought for equal rights for Black people—and all Americans.

The civil rights activists marched over this bridge in Selma, Alabama, in 1965. Police attacked the unarmed marchers.

MAKING MOVIES

In 1990, Ava graduated from high school. When it was time for college, she went to the University of California, Los Angeles (UCLA). There, she studied English and African American studies. Soon after, Ava got a job at CBS News and as a publicist. In 1999, she started her own company, The DuVernay Agency. Ava worked for movies and TV shows. This is when Ava first became interested in directing films.

The University of California at Los Angeles (UCLA)

During her Christmas holiday in 2005, Ava used $6,000 in savings to make a short film called *Saturday Night Life*. Only 12 minutes long, the film was based on her mother's experiences. It followed a single mom and her three kids shopping at a discount store. The film got the attention of critics.

Ava as a young filmmaker

Ava did not pick up a film camera until she was 32 years old!

11

Ava then turned to making documentary films. In 2007, she directed *Compton in C Minor* about her hometown of Compton, California. According to Ava, the concept for the film was "to capture Compton in only two hours and present whatever she found." The next year, she made a documentary about hip-hop in Los Angeles. It was called *This Is the Life*. Many considered it a must-see movie.

This Is the Life follows a group of hip-hop artists and friends.

"I LOVE THE STORIES THAT I'M TELLING."
—AVA DUVERNAY

Ava behind the camera on a film set

In 2010, Ava wrote and directed a drama called *I Will Follow*. The movie was about her aunt after she got cancer. "I was a caregiver for my aunt, Denise Sexton, in the last year and a half of her life," said Ava. Film critic Roger Ebert called it "one of the best films I've seen about coming to terms with the death of a loved one."

In 2011, Ava wrote and directed another movie that was close to her heart. *Middle of Nowhere* follows a Black woman who drops out of school to support her incarcerated (in-KAHR-suh-reyt-tid) husband. Ava shows both the husband and wife as victims of an unfair system. Or, as Ava put it, "the life that families live as invisible prisoners."

Ava stands in front of *Middle of Nowhere* poster at the movie's premiere.

"THE LIVES OF BLACK PEOPLE, OUR VERY BREATH, OUR VERY DIGNITY, OUR VERY HUMANITY, ARE VALUABLE AND MATTER TO THE WORLD."
—AVA DUVERNAY

Ava won best director award at the Sundance Film Festival for *Middle of Nowhere*.

"The idea of looking at the victims of incarceration—the mothers, sisters, and daughters—really came out of knowing women who were going through it," said Ava. Film professor Michael T. Martin called Ava's work, "a call to action." He also described her as the "**vanguard** of a new **generation** of Black filmmakers."

To be incarcerated means to be held in a prison. The United States incarcerates more people than any other nation in the world. This is called mass incarceration. Not everyone is treated equally in this country. As a result, there are many more people of color in prison.

Ava working on the set of *Selma*

Inspired by Ava's summers in Selma, Louisiana, she went on to direct a movie called *Selma*. The film covers the 1965 civil rights marches her father witnessed. It features Dr. Martin Luther King Jr. and other civil rights leaders. *Selma* was released in 2015 before the 50th anniversary of the marches. The movie was a big hit. It was nominated for many awards, including two Oscars and four Golden Globes.

"THE GOAL IS TO SHOW THE DIFFERENT DIMENSIONS OF US."
—AVA DUVERNAY

After *Selma*, Ava was invited to direct Marvel's *Black Panther*. But she said no. "We had different ideas about what the story would be," Ava later said. Ava then made a documentary called *13th*. Some critics would call it her most important movie.

Colman Domingo
(Schauspieler /Actor)

Ava DuVernay
(Regisseurin/Director)

David Oyelowo
(Schauspieler /Actor)

Selma was the first major movie about Dr. Martin Luther King Jr.

The film *13th* is about racism, justice, and mass incarceration. The title is based on the U.S. Constitution's Thirteenth Amendment, which outlawed slavery. The movie forces viewers to look at American history with clear eyes. It lays out how the unfair treatment of Black Americans led to the incarceration of more than 2 million people. Ava urges the people watching *13th* to take action to change the system.

Ava and the musician Common at the opening of *13th*

"THE WHOLE FILM IS A **VIRTUAL** TOUR THROUGH RACISM."
—AVA DUVERNAY

In 2018, Ava directed a very different kind of movie. The film is based on the young adult novel, *A Wrinkle in Time*. It follows Meg Murray, a young girl who travels through space and time to save her father.

Ava picked Storm Reid, a young Black actress, to star in *A Wrinkle in Time*.

Madeleine L'Engle wrote *A Wrinkle in Time* in 1962.

AVA'S IMPACT

> "DON'T BELIEVE EVERYTHING YOU THINK. . . . CHALLENGE AND
> EXPAND YOUR VIEW OF THE WORLD AND YOUR EXPERIENCES."
> —AVA DUVERNAY

Ava DuVernay continues to create films that make a difference. "I'm honored to be making art during this time," said Ava. And she's proud to see other Black people making great art too. Artists of color are expressing themselves and telling their *own* stories. Ava believes everyone must play a part in changing the world for the better. "I want people to be having their own conversation about it," she said. "That's my great hope."

Ava is a huge inspiration to many Black women and girls. She founded ARRAY to support young filmmakers of color.

In addition to being a filmmaker, Ava also creates and directs TV shows. One is called *Queen Sugar*. Ava hired 35 women directors to work on the show, including groundbreaking filmmaker Julie Dash.

FILMOGRAPHY

AVA'S FEATURE MOVIES

2008	*This Is the Life*
2010	*I Will Follow*
2012	*Middle of Nowhere*
2014	*Selma*
2016	*13th*
2018	*A Wrinkle in Time*

GLOSSARY

activist (AK-tuh-vist) a person who fights for a cause

amendment (uh-MEND-muhnt) a new rule added to the U.S. Constitution

cancer (KAN-sur) a serious, often deadly, disease that destroys parts of the body

civil rights (SIV-uhl RITES) the rights everyone should have to freedom and equal treatment under the law, regardless of who they are

critics (KRIT-iks) people who judge or criticize something

dignity (DIG-nuh-tee) a sense of honor and self-respect

dimensions (dih-MEN-shuhns) aspects or features of someone or something

documentary (dok-yuh-MEN-tuh-ree) a movie that recreates actual events or true-life stories

generation (jen-uh-RAY-shuhn) a group of people born around the same time

humanity (hyoo-MAN-uh-tee) kindness and sympathy

Jim Crow laws (GYM KROW LAWZ) unjust laws in the Southern United States that kept Black people separate and prevented them from voting and living in certain places, for example

justice (JUHSS-tiss) fairness

nominated (NOM-uh-neyt-uhd) formally selected to win an award

publicist (PUHB-luh-sist) a person who makes something widely known

racism (REY-siz-uhm) a system of beliefs and policies based on the idea that one race is better than another

vanguard (VAN-gahrd) the leader of a movement

virtual (VUR-choo-ul) for all practical purposes

witnessed (WIT-nissd) saw something

FIND OUT MORE

BOOKS

Blofield, Robert. *How to Make a Movie in 10 Easy Lessons*. Mission Viejo, CA: Walter Foster Publishing, 2015.

Frost, Shelley. *Kids Guide to Movie Making*. New York, NY: Amazon KDP, 2020.

Willoughby, Nick. *Digital Filmmaking for Kids*. Hoboken, NJ: John Wiley & Sons, 2015.

WEBSITES

ARRAY
https://arraynow.com

Britannica Kids: Ava DuVernay
https://kids.britannica.com/students/article/Ava-DuVernay/630857

UCLA Lab School: Ava DuVernay
https://www.labschool.ucla.edu/teach/black-history-american-history/ava-duvernay/

INDEX

ABOUT THE AUTHORS

Joyce Markovics has written hundreds of books for kids. Movies have helped shaped her outlook on life and inspired her to tell stories. She's grateful to all people who have beaten the odds to make great art. Joyce would like to dedicate this book to Sarah Rockett.

Alrick A. Brown is a storyteller and an Assistant Professor at NYU who uses filmmaking to touch the hearts and challenge the minds of his audiences. His creativity is shaped by his time living and working in West Africa, his upbringing in New Jersey, and his travels around the world.

COUNTING
Is for the

Birds

Frank Mazzola, Jr.

SCHOLASTIC INC.
New York Toronto London Auckland Sydney
Mexico City New Delhi Hong Kong

For Cindy,
my best friend and
bird-watching partner

I wish to thank the following people for their encouragement and support:
my parents, Frank and Gidge, and Juliana.

I also want to thank: Holly and the Massachusetts Audubon Society for lending me the bird mounts;
Betty and Diane for reviewing the manuscript; Mary Ann for her interest in the book; Kelly and Yolanda
for their assistance; Pam for her insight; Jiggs the cat for inspiration;
and Jerry for getting me hooked on children's books.

ISBN 0-439-15105-8

12 11 10 9 8 7 6 5 4 3 2   0 1 2 3 4 5/0

Printed in the U.S.A.   14

First Scholastic printing, April 2000

The illustrations in this book are digital paintings created using a
personal computer. They were painted on-screen using a Wacom tablet
and wireless pen. No photography was used.

The text is set in Adobe Galahad.

Designed by Frank Mazzola, Jr.

The feeder is still,
    it hangs overhead.
It's morning and time
    for birds to be fed.
This new day begins
    with fog all around.
Be still because there
    are birds to be found.

O

Well hidden below,
　　a cat lies in wait.
This cat is greedy,
　　his appetite great.
He sees there are **zero**
　　birds he can catch,
No birds on the feeder
　　for him to snatch.

striped sunflower

black-oiled sunflower

safflower

white millet

The bird feeder in this book contains four kinds of seeds: black-oiled and striped sunflower, safflower, and white millet. This seed medley attracts a wide variety of birds. From black-capped chickadees to blue jays, these birds visit the feeder in search of food.

1   2

Then one chickadee
    grabs on with his feet.
A second floats in,
    her tiny wings beat.
Both birds move quickly,
    so keep them in view.
Count them together
    and you will find two.

These two acrobats are black-capped chickadees. When chickadees feed at a feeder, they take turns. The dominant or stronger bird eats first while the other chickadees wait close by for their turn.

3   4

Three is a titmouse,
    and four is her mate.
These birds are feeding
    at a rapid rate.
These little creatures
    will flee to the trees.
Once they have landed,
    they peck at the seeds.

The tufted titmouse is a relative of the chickadee. Titmice take just one seed at a time and then fly off to the trees. In the safety of the trees, they eat the seed. It is fun to count the number of times chickadees and titmice return to the feeder for more seeds.

5 6

Bird five clutches on
　　and pecks with his beak.
Number six arrives
　　and takes a quick peek.
These woodpeckers eat bugs
　　they find in wood.
They also eat seeds,
　　which taste really good.

Ladybug

Elder borer

Eastern eyed
click beetle

Downy woodpeckers enjoy eating sunflower seeds, even though insects are their favorite food. They use their powerful beaks to find bugs in tree trunks, branches, and bark. Have you ever heard an erratic tapping sound outside? This may be a downy looking for an insect meal.

7   8

Birds seven and eight
        drop in from up high.
Goldfinches' feathers
        help color the sky.
The number of birds
        grows larger so fast,
The cat still watches
        the birds that fly past.

Like all finches, American goldfinches have conical-shaped beaks that are designed for eating seeds. The conical shape enables the finch to hold on to and crack a seed without using its feet.

9   10

Nine is a sparrow,
    who dives in with speed.
The tenth comes along
    and follows her lead.
Ten birds are feeding,
    with plenty to share.
Eating together,
    enjoying the fare.

☐ Summer

■ Winter

American tree sparrows are migratory and travel in flocks of up to fifty birds.
In the summer, they live in Alaska and northern Canada. In the fall, they
migrate to southern Canada and to parts of the United States, where they
spend the winter.

11   12

Eleven is red,
> he feeds on the ground.

Number twelve swoops in,
> not making a sound.

Crouching in silence,
> the cat keeps his stare,

While cardinals feed
> in front of his lair.

Hopper feeder

Platform feeder

All three methods
will attract ground–
feeding birds.

Seeds tossed
on the ground

Northern cardinals usually feed on the ground and occasionally dine at hanging feeders. During the mating season, the male cardinal brings a seed to the female. If the female accepts the seed, the male and female become mates. This is called mate feeding.

13   14

A famished duo
    is next to arrive.
Thirteen and fourteen,
    these finches will thrive.
Fourteen birds feasting,
    all eating their fill.
Each bird is hungry
    and cracks seeds with skill.

Look, no teeth!

Like all birds, purple finches swallow their food whole because they do not have teeth. Birds have a special muscle in their stomach that grinds the food so that it can be digested. This muscle is called the gizzard.

15   16

Bird fifteen flies by,

his pal sweeps in, too.

These buntings are colored

indigo blue.

Sixteen birds eating

and looking about,

Devouring seeds

until they run out.

Indigo buntings are shy birds and rarely venture far from the underbrush that protects them. They eat small seeds, weed seeds, and insects. Scattering white millet on the ground near the underbrush may lure them out into view.

17   18

Seventeen and eighteen
join this array.
These two nuthatches
will soon fly away.
For now they relax
and wait for the chance
To feed on the seeds
they eye with a glance.

Nuthatches, or upside-down birds, are the only common birds that can walk
headfirst down tree trunks. Unlike woodpeckers, the white-breasted
nuthatch does not use its tail for support when climbing. By moving one
strong foot at a time, the nuthatch can move up and down the tree trunk
without falling off.

19

The feeder twists when

a blue jay flies in.

Number nineteen enjoys

this swift side spin.

He seems imposing

because of his size.

The others react

with utter surprise.

Blue jay

Black-capped chickadee

Blue jays often scare smaller birds at the feeder. Jays are much larger and need more room to land. Aggressive behavior is common in all birds, but because the blue jay is twice the size of the smaller birds, its arrival usually causes a disturbance.

20

The second blue jay,
  the final bird here,
Is looking around
  and showing no fear.
Our count is twenty,
  it's time for the feast.
Twenty is plenty
  for this sneaky beast.

Blue jays eat sunflower seeds from the feeder but prefer acorns. In the fall when acorns are available, blue jays pick off the caps with their beaks and eat the nutmeat they find inside. Like squirrels, blue jays also hide extra acorns for future meals.

Launching himself with
    his prey well in sight,
The cat tries to catch
    the birds in midflight.
But something goes wrong,
    a gray streak lands here,
Scaring his quarry
    that used to be near.

Squirrels are a constant menace to bird feeders. In an attempt to get to the seeds quicker, squirrels often chew the wood or plastic feeder. One good way to keep them off your feeder is to hang it eight feet away from branches and six feet above the ground.

20

One selfish squirrel

    spoiled all the cat's fun.

And as you can see,

    his plan is now done.

The cat feels sad

    because he missed a treat—

Twenty birds are now

    feeding down the street.

It is estimated that over one hundred billion birds live on earth. That means there are more birds than people. We are surrounded by birds! Hang a feeder and birds will come to feed—you can count on it!

A guide to the birds in this book

Black-capped chickadee   1   2

Has a black cap and bib.
The male and female look similar.

Tufted titmouse   3   4

A small gray bird with a tufted crest.
Both the male and female
look alike.

Downy woodpecker   5   6

These birds look similar with the exception of the male's red
patch of feathers
behind his head.

American goldfinch   7   8

In the summer, the female's feathers
are duller than the male's. This
difference helps the female blend
into the environment, which is
important when she is sitting
on her nest.

American tree sparrow   9   10

Is identified by a single dark spot on its
chest, solid reddish brown cap,
gray face and chest, and a beak
that is dark on top and yellow
on the bottom. Both the male
and female look the same.

Northern cardinal   11   12

The male is red and the
female is olive brown with
red highlights. The female's
color helps hide her when she
is sitting on her nest. Both
have red beaks.

Purple finch   13   14

The male has a raspberry color on
his head, back, belly, and rump,
and the female is brown and
white with brown stripes going
down her chest and belly.

Indigo bunting   15   16

The male is a brilliant blue. The
female is drab in color. A predator
will have difficulty locating her when
she is sitting on her nest.

White-breasted nuthatch   17   18

These birds look alike with
the exception of the male's
black cap.

Blue jay   19   20

A blue bird with a crest,
white spots on tail and
wings, and a black neck
band. The male and female
look similar.